Taylor Swift
A NEW ERA

T0077145

TRIUMPH
BOOKS

KATY SPRINKEL

Library of Congress Cataloging-in-Publication Data is available upon request.

This book is available in quantity at special discounts for your group or organization. For further information, contact:

Triumph Books LLC
814 North Franklin Street
Chicago, Illinois 60610
(312) 337-0747
www.triumphbooks.com

Printed in U.S.A.

ISBN: 978-1-63727-682-2

Design by Patricia Frey
Edited by Laine Morreau

Contents

CHAPTER 1

Superstar

7

CHAPTER 2

Teardrops on My Guitar

13

CHAPTER 3

ME!

27

CHAPTER 4

Speak Now

55

CHAPTER 5

Bejeweled

67

CHAPTER 6

New Romantics

79

CHAPTER 7

Sparks Fly

89

CHAPTER 8

Our Song

99

CHAPTER 9

Mastermind

111

CHAPTER 10

End Game

123

chapter 1
SUPERSTAR

Greatness honors greatness. Taylor speaks at Carole King's second induction ceremony into the Rock and Roll Hall of Fame in 2021.

14

With *The Tortured Poets Department*, Taylor Swift took her fourteenth consecutive album to No. 1 on the Billboard charts, making her the only female artist to achieve the feat and trailing only the Beatles, who have nineteen.

Are there any worlds Taylor Swift has yet to conquer? She's an electrifying performer who sells out arenas around the globe. She's a prolific songwriter and musician with an uncanny knack for reinvention. She's an influencer who uses her enormous platform to inspire and unite, and a musician who exerts her influence to reshape the entire industry for the better. Taylor Swift is more than just a musical artist. She is an *icon*. She's a force of nature who has reached the summit of musical success by doing the most outlandish thing of all: being herself. She's one of the most successful musical artists not just today but in history.

Given all that, it's almost impossible to imagine that there could have been another gear, but Taylor found it. She had not one but three albums hit No. 1 on the Billboard 200 chart in 2023: her new release, *Midnights*, along with her rerecordings *Speak Now* and *1989*, the latter of which was the best-selling album of the year among all artists. *The Tortured Poets Department*, released in April 2024, unsurprisingly shot straight to No. 1 as well. Her Eras Tour, which is still ongoing, shattered records, already becoming the most successful live tour in history by an unthinkable margin. And her concert film *Taylor Swift: The Eras Tour* became the highest-grossing concert or performance film of all time. She won her fourth Grammy for Album of the Year in 2024 too, for *Midnights*— becoming the only artist ever to have done so in the Grammys' sixty-six-year history. She was the most streamed artist globally on both Spotify and Apple Music. She was named Billboard's Greatest Pop Star of 2023, and *Time*'s prestigious Person of the Year. Oh, and she became a billionaire with a *B*.

As *Billboard* put it, "She is on a level of pop stardom right now that no other contemporary artist is even

Taylor performs onstage during the Eras Tour at Estadio Olimpico Nilton Santos on November 17, 2023, in Rio de Janeiro.

approaching, and remarkably few would be able to hold onto if they ever got there."

Her dominance as a pop artist is unprecedented. She's the rare artist whose fans span multiple generations in equal measure, from Gen X and millennials to Gen Z and now Alpha. Known collectively as Swifties, her fans are a powerful force, capable of doing the unthinkable—putting an entire album's worth of songs in the Billboard top 10, collectively creating enough seismic activity to register on the Richter scale (as they did at one Eras concert), and even spiking local and national economies (which they did basically everywhere the Eras Tour landed). And the Swifties get as good as they give; it's impossible to think of another artist who gives more back to her fans than Taylor.

Put it all together, and it's hard to make the argument that Taylor Swift is *not* the GOAT. Where she goes next is anyone's guess, but at just thirty-four years old, there's still a lot of beautiful music yet to be written. ★

"She's the last monoculture left in our stratified world."

—*Time*, proclaiming Swift as its 2023 Person of the Year

chapter 2

TEARDROPS ON MY GUITAR

Taylor, shown here in 2009, is never far from a guitar.

Every Swiftie knows that Taylor feels most at home when she's writing music—whether that's at her piano, strumming a melody on the guitar, or in the studio with her trusted collaborators.

She refers to songwriting as a calling, and it's something that she practices daily. From the beginning of her career to now, the approach has been the same: she follows the song where it takes her.

Unlike many artists, Taylor is not opaque about her songwriting process. On the contrary—she's extremely forthcoming with her fans, giving them incredible access into how her musical mind works. She often shares social media posts with glimpses of her creative process: videos, recorded voice memos, writing, studio experimentation, and more.

Inspiration can come from anywhere at any time, and harnessing it can be like capturing lightning in a bottle. Ideas can often be inconvenient—waking her up in the middle of the night to hastily scribble down a snatch of a lyric. They can also be persistent—such as a little

> "She's like a whole room of writers as one person, with that voice and charisma. She's everything at once."
>
> —Phoebe Bridgers

piece of a melody that keeps coming back again and again until it's fully formed. Taylor has a couple bulletproof strategies for capturing the moment. One of her songwriting secret weapons: her phone. When an idea comes to her, the first thing she'll usually do is grab her phone and record a voice memo of herself singing a hook or a piece of a melody. Or she'll tap out a snatch of a lyric as a note to herself. She also uses her phone to store stray ideas that don't have a context yet. An avid reader, she also keeps lists of words that pique her interest. And she writes down bits of conversation she hears out in the world and phrases that, with a little tweak, might just be the focus of a song someday.

More often than not, though, the kernel of a song starts with the melody, which has led to her second strategy: at home or on the road, she's never far from a piano or a guitar, so she can work out a song's structure on the fly.

And once a melody is in place, Taylor typically starts chipping away at the lyrics. Maybe the chorus comes first, or maybe the verse; whatever the case, she is fastidious about each and every word, working and reworking each phrase until she is satisfied. Her attention to detail is legendary. And she is ruthless with herself—if it isn't working, it's out. She'll change lyrics up at the last second, or throw big chunks of a song out completely. She'll fret over a single word in the chorus, mulling it over and over until the delivery has *just* the right inflection. What comes across is the true joy of creation in all its messiness and chaos.

But ultimately there is no exact formula. The path a song takes is different every time. Sometimes the whole song comes spilling out in one giant gush. Other times, a concept can take years. "We Are Never Getting Back Together" and "Tim McGraw" each took less than a half hour to complete; "All Too Well," on the other hand, took years.

The Write Stuff

Accepting honors for Songwriter-Artist of the Decade at the Nashville Songwriter Awards in 2022, Taylor perfectly described how her writing style falls into three distinct categories. She explained that there are three types of songs and three metaphorical "pens" with which she writes them.

The first type of song, a **fountain pen** song, paints "a vivid picture of a situation, down to the chipped paint on the doorframe and the incense dust on the vinyl shelf." Drilling down into the details to color in the lines of a story is a common practice for Taylor, and you can hear it reflected in songs from "Our Song" to "Lavender Haze."

The second type is the **quill pen** song, such as the Shakespearean "Love Story," in which "the words and phrasings are antiquated" like "a letter written by Emily Dickinson's great-grandmother while sewing a lace curtain."

Then there's the brilliantly termed **glitter gel pen** song—pop confections such as "Shake It Off": "Frivolous, carefree, bouncy, syncopated perfectly to the beat. Glitter gel pen lyrics don't care if you don't take them seriously, because they don't take themselves seriously.... It's what we need every once in a while in these fraught times in which we live."

Taylor's songwriting
secret weapon: her
phone.

Taylor worked closely with cowriter Liz Rose on her first two albums, *Taylor Swift* and *Fearless*.

The process of songwriting can be ephemeral or elusive; Taylor has likened her musical ideas to puffy, glittery clouds that float by. The trick is to have the discipline to capture them when they come. And it's not just about the idea; it's about what she does with it afterward. "Creativity is getting inspiration and having that lightning-bolt idea moment and then having the hard-work ethic to sit down at the desk and write it down," she told *Vogue.*

Music is her lifeblood—the way she works out her own problems, the way she expresses herself and leaves her mark on the world. In an interview with Jam! Music, she said, "I write songs to help me understand life a little more. I write songs to get past things that cause me pain. And I write songs because sometimes life makes more sense to me when it's being sung in a chorus, and when I can write in a verse."

It's hard to believe it now, but there was once a time when people complained that Taylor got too personal with her

Did You Know?

The prodigious songwriter Nils Sjöberg is none other than Taylor Swift herself!

lyrics, that she was putting too much of her own problems and experiences onto the page. But it's precisely this vulnerability and honesty that resonate with listeners. As one twenty-year-old Swiftie put it to *Time,* Taylor's music connects because it speaks to the authentic and universal human experience: "When I listen to her songs, I think about what I've been through—not what she's been through."

Taylor has said that music is not only a way to process her own feelings, but it

> **"[A] song can defy logic or time. A good song transports you to your truest feelings and translates those feelings for you. A good song stays with you even when people or feelings don't."**
>
> —Taylor in 2022

Taylor with longtime collaborator and producer Jack Antonoff. "Sometimes, he sits at the piano and we both just start ad-libbing and the song seems to create itself," she told the *New York Times.* "His excitement and exuberance about writing songs is contagious."

gives her a forum to say what she wants to say in the most elegant and straightforward way. "The reason why I keep doing it is because it's like a message in a bottle," she told the *New York Times.* "You can put this message in a bottle, throw it out into the ocean, and maybe someday, the person that you wrote that song about is going to hear it and understand exactly how you felt.... It's conveying a message to someone that's more real than what you had the courage to say in person."

Indeed, Taylor's honesty, sensitivity, and talent in turning life's triumphs and miseries into song have consistently inspired audiences. And the fact that she's writing about her own life? Well, she'd be quick to admit it, sure...but she'd also point out that so does every songwriter, everywhere, since time immemorial.

Eleven albums—including two full-length offerings during the pandemic (but not including multiple *Taylor's Versions* and the *TPD Anthology*)—prove what everyone not living under a rock already knows: Taylor was born to make music. It's what drives her, what feeds her soul, and ultimately what brings her the most joy.

"There's a common misconception that artists have to be miserable in order to make good art, that art and suffering go hand in hand," she reflected to the *New York Times* in 2022. "I'm really grateful to have learned this isn't true." ★

Say What?

With such complex lyrics, it's inevitable that listeners might mistake a phrase or two along the way. Here are a handful of the funniest misheard lyrics from the Taylor Swift canon, as shared by Swifties.

The song: "Wildest Dreams"

Maybe you heard: He's so dull, and handsome as hell.

But the real lyrics are: He's so tall, and handsome as hell.

The song: "Blank Space"

Maybe you heard: All the lonely Starbucks lovers.

But the real lyrics are: Got a long list of ex-lovers.

The song: "Cruel Summer"

Maybe you heard: He looks so pretty, like a devil.

But the real lyrics are: He looks up, grinning like a devil.

The song: "I Knew You Were Trouble."

Maybe you heard: And the stratosphere comes creeping in.

But the real lyrics are: And the saddest fear comes creeping in.

The song: "Mr. Perfectly Fine"

Maybe you heard: It takes everything in me just to get a beach day.

But the real lyrics are: It takes everything in me just to get up each day.

The song: "Starlight"

Maybe you heard: I'm a Barbie on the boardwalk, summer of '45.

But the real lyrics are: I met Bobby on the boardwalk, summer of '45.

The song: "Bejeweled"

Maybe you heard: I miss you, but I miss Spider-Man.

But the real lyrics are: I miss you, but I miss sparkling.

"Getting a great idea with songwriting is a lot like love. You don't know why this one is different, but it is. You don't know why this one is better, but it is. It sticks in your head, and you can't stop thinking about it."

chapter 3
ME!

TAYLOR SWIFT

"[Songwriters are people] who love the craft. Who live for that rare, pure moment when a magical cloud floats down right in front of you in the form of an idea for a song, and all you have to do is grab it. Then shape it like clay. Prune it like a garden. And then wish on every lucky star or pray to whatever power you believe in that it might find its way out into the world and make someone feel seen, feel understood, feel joined in their grief or heartbreak or joy for just a moment."

—Taylor accepting Songwriter-Artist of the Decade Award honors at the 2022 Nashville Songwriter Awards

It's hard to describe the sum total of an artist's artistic output in broad strokes, but it's even more impossible with someone as nimble and ever changing as Taylor Swift. Taylor is an artist who consistently defies expectations—an artist constantly reaching for something more, better, different.

Changing lanes is risky for a singer. Experiment too much and you could lose fans expecting more of the same. Don't change enough and you're accused of being one-note. But Taylor has walked that tightrope beautifully. Her knack for reinvention is masterful, and the breadth and depth of her own musical influences are always growing. It's a testament to her authenticity as an artist and her commitment to her own craft.

As prolific music critic Chuck Klosterman put it, writing about Swift, that craft is at the heart of the matter: "There's simply no antecedent for this kind of career: a cross-genre, youth-oriented, critically acclaimed colossus based entirely on the intuitive songwriting merits of a single female artist."

From the country-inflected paeans to teen romance off her self-titled debut album to the intricately crafted, genre-hopping offerings of *Midnights*, her 2023–24 world tour has celebrated all ten of the artist's distinct so-called eras in her career. Here's a brief tour through the eras, from 2006 to the present, including her latest evolution, 2024's *The Tortured Poets Department.* ★

Through the Eras, Taylor has delivered consistently excellent music.

Putting out her own first record as a teenager, Taylor's debut album, *Taylor Swift*, spooled out almost like the pages of her diary. Listeners heard firsthand the heartache and hopefulness that peppered her young life. Two of that album's gems portray different sides of the breakup coin with deft precision. While "Tim McGraw" is a bittersweet send-off to a lost relationship, "Picture to Burn" is more of a fired-up, get-lost anthem.

The gawky girl with the guitar and the blonde ringlet curls became an instant darling in the country music world. She also got the attention of critics, who were widely supportive of the new artist. The *New York Times* described *Taylor Swift* as nothing less than "a small masterpiece of pop-minded country."

This first era is unmistakably country-tinged, with cowboy boots, heavy eyeliner, and Taylor's long, curly 'do.

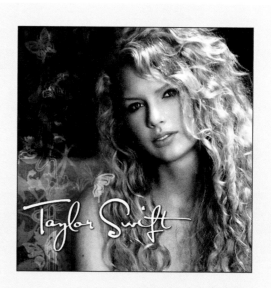

Release date: October 24, 2006

Track list:
1. Tim McGraw
2. Picture to Burn
3. Teardrops on My Guitar
4. A Place in This World
5. Cold as You
6. The Outside
7. Tied Together with a Smile
8. Stay Beautiful
9. Should've Said No
10. Mary's Song (Oh My My My)
11. Our Song

Fun Fact: Did you ever wonder what Tim McGraw song Taylor was singing about on the opening track? It's "Can't Tell Me Nothin'," a rollicking tribute to the virtues of stubbornness, off McGraw's smash *Live Like You Were Dying*. Recounting writing the song "Tim McGraw" to the *Nashville Scene* in 2006, Swift recalled, "It's about how a lot of people will warn you not to do stuff, but you're gonna have to figure it out yourself by making your own mistakes, no matter what advice anybody gives you."

Fearless

Fans of country music were already well acquainted with Taylor, but *Fearless* made her a crossover success with songs such as "Love Story" and "You Belong with Me" seeing extensive airplay on pop radio. (They peaked at No. 2 and No. 4, respectively, on the Billboard Hot 100.) Suddenly everyone knew the tall girl with the curly blonde hair and the glittery guitar.

She won four Grammys for the effort at the 52nd Annual Grammy Awards in 2010, including Album of the Year. *L* magazine's Tom Breihan wrote, "There might be someone out there making better pop music right now, but I sure haven't heard her."

The *Fearless* era was Taylor's high-water mark for girly dresses (accessorized with cowboy boots, of course) and an eye-popping amount of glitter. Reflecting upon the album in 2021, she wrote on Instagram: "*Fearless* was an album full of magic and curiosity, the bliss and devastation of youth. It was the diary of the adventures and explorations of a teenage girl who was learning tiny lessons with every new crack in the facade of the fairy-tale ending she'd been shown in the movies."

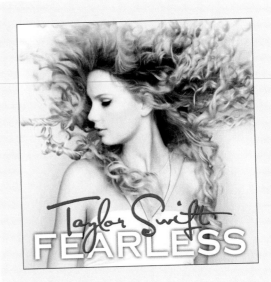

Release date: November 8, 2008

Track list:

1. Fearless
2. Fifteen
3. Love Story
4. Hey Stephen
5. White Horse
6. You Belong with Me
7. Breathe
8. Tell Me Why
9. You're Not Sorry
10. The Way I Loved You
11. Forever & Always
12. The Best Day
13. Change

Fun Fact: Sure, *Fearless* won Album of the Year at the Grammys (Taylor's first of four to date) and is the most awarded album in country music history, but it was *this* achievement that brought Taylor to tears: getting "White Horse" on *Grey's Anatomy*. "I have never been that excited," she told *Billboard*. "My love of *Grey's Anatomy* has never wavered. It's my longest relationship to date."

Speak Now

Despite the fact that Taylor had earned serious street cred from overwhelming critical and popular success—including a highly coveted Grammy for Album of the Year—there were still doubters who felt she could be a gimmick, or that she rested on the laurels of the more experienced cowriters who had contributed to her albums. *Speak Now* answered those doubters head-on: Taylor holds sole songwriting credit for every single track on it.

Awarding the album four out of four stars, *Rolling Stone* wrote, "Swift's third album...is roughly twice as good as 2008's *Fearless*, which was roughly twice as good as her 2006 debut."

The *Speak Now* era is Taylor's most romantic era, defined by the theatricality of its music and staging. (Who can forget that enormous lighted tree?)

Gone were the cowboy boots and sequins as she embraced a more classic femininity, with loose curls and flowing, diaphanous dresses along with elegant ensembles (including the one pictured opposite) befitting a more mature look for the then–nineteen-year-old.

Release date: October 25, 2010

Track list:

1. Mine
2. Sparks Fly
3. Back to December
4. Speak Now
5. Dear John
6. Mean
7. The Story of Us
8. Never Grow Up
9. Enchanted
10. Better Than Revenge
11. Innocent
12. Haunted
13. Last Kiss
14. Long Live

Fun Fact: Each song on *Speak Now* is about a specific person—famous, unfamous, and (in the case of Kanye West, on "Innocent") infamous. "Every single song is like a road map to what that relationship stood for," Taylor told Yahoo! Music in 2010.

Red

The *Red* era was all about romance, romance, romance! Characterized first and foremost by the color red: it was ever present in her stage outfits and, of course, in her signature red lipstick. Taylor embraced a preppier aesthetic in her style, with cozy fall layers, textured knits, and hats. (She gives away a hat to a young fan during each performance of *Red*'s "22" on the Eras Tour.) She also unveiled a pretty major hair transformation, straightening her curly locks and sporting bangs for the first time.

Unfairly or not, *Red* will always be remembered as a breakup album. And indeed, it rises and falls on the genuine heartbreak that fueled the songs here. Fans and critics were here for it: "Lyrically, it's...deeper and a little darker.... Musically, it's bigger and bolder than anything she's ever done in the pop world," wrote *Entertainment Weekly*, awarding it a B+. *Slant* magazine presciently wrote that *Red* boasted "career-best work for Swift, who now sounds like the pop star she was destined to be all along."

Fun Fact: "All Too Well" has long been a fan favorite. But when Taylor mentioned that the song was originally written to be ten minutes long, it became *legend*. The full version was released on 2022's *Red (Taylor's Version)* and instantly shot to the top spot on the charts, becoming the longest song ever to reach No. 1 on the Billboard Hot 100.

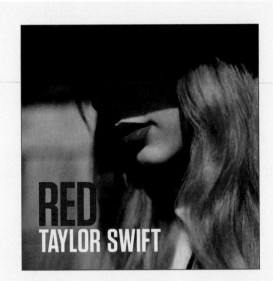

Release date: October 22, 2012

Track list:

1. State of Grace
2. Red
3. Treacherous
4. I Knew You Were Trouble.
5. All Too Well
6. 22
7. I Almost Do
8. We Are Never Ever Getting Back Together
9. Stay Stay Stay
10. The Last Time
11. Holy Ground
12. Sad Beautiful Tragic
13. The Lucky One
14. Everything Has Changed
15. Starlight
16. Begin Again

1989

This was Taylor Swift's supermodel era. She moved to New York, hung with her squad (many of whom were famous models), and leveled up her fashion game. With paparazzi at her doorstep every day, she served up look after high-fashion look. Think: lots of heels and stacked Oxfords, sharp coats, designer separates, and a sleek bob to match.

There is not a trace of country music on *1989*. It is a pure pop album, and this perhaps more than any record cemented Taylor's status as a musical titan. It is filled with countless hits, including tracks such as "Shake It Off" and "Blank Space," both of which poke at Taylor's haters. She spoke in 2019 about how intense criticism spurred her to keep stretching herself—to prove people wrong about who she was...and wasn't. "I decided I would be what they said I couldn't be," she said.

"By making pop with almost no contemporary references, Ms. Swift is aiming somewhere even higher, a mode of timelessness that few true pop stars...even bother aspiring to," heralded the *New York Times*. "Everyone else striving to sound like now will have to shift gears once the now sound changes. But not Ms. Swift, who's waging, and winning, a new war, one she'd never admit to fighting."

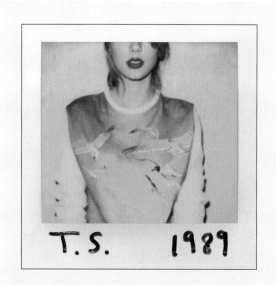

Release date: October 27, 2014

Track list:
1. Welcome to New York
2. Blank Space
3. Style
4. Out of the Woods
5. All You Had to Do Was Stay
6. Shake It Off
7. I Wish You Would
8. Bad Blood
9. Wildest Dreams
10. How You Get the Girl
11. This Love
12. I Know Places
13. Clean

Fun Fact: One of Taylor's most iconic songs of all time, "Blank Space," was years in the making. She put it together line by line, "like a crossword puzzle," from lines she wrote and collected over the years, many of them in response to how the media portrayed her. Bonus fun fact: the song shot to No. 1 on the Billboard Hot 100, replacing "Shake It Off." In doing so, Taylor became the first female artist ever to unseat herself at the top spot.

Reputation

"I'm sorry, but the old Taylor can't come to the phone right now / Why? Oh, 'cause she's dead." With those words from "Look What You Made Me Do," Taylor put an exclamation point on her latest reinvention. *Reputation* was a declaration of independence: she was freeing herself from the shackles of toxic criticism for good. This record is full of edge, defiance, and a healthy dose of revenge. Gone is the romantic, frilly Taylor of old; this version of Taylor is brash, bold, and unwilling to back down from a fight.

The aesthetics of the *Reputation* era were similarly provocative: dark makeup, black sequins, knee-high boots, and lots and lots of snakes.

The *Los Angeles Times* heralded it as "her most focused, most cohesive album to date," and the *Guardian* called it "a master class of pop songwriting." *Spin* wrote in its rave review, "Never has she sounded freer than she does here, a self-styled villain biting the forbidden fruit of gossip and letting its juices run down her neck."

Fun Fact: In its debut week, *Reputation* sold more albums than every other album on the Billboard 200 *combined.*

Release date: November 10, 2017

Track list:
1. ...Ready for It?
2. End Game
3. I Did Something Bad
4. Don't Blame Me
5. Delicate
6. Look What You Made Me Do
7. So It Goes...
8. Gorgeous
9. Getaway Car
10. King of My Heart
11. Dancing with Our Hands Tied
12. Dress
13. This Is Why We Can't Have Nice Things
14. Call It What You Want
15. New Year's Day

Lover

The pastel-tinged world of *Lover* is a universe away from *Reputation*, and a softer, sweeter style accompanies the record. The visuals include lots of pretty pastels, as well as the kaleidoscopic rainbows of songs like "ME!" A celebration of romantic bliss, songs range from the intimate, sultry title track to the ebullient "You Need to Calm Down," a sly takedown of bigots. Taylor described the album to *Vogue* as "a love letter to love, in all of its maddening, passionate, exciting, enchanting, horrific, tragic, wonderful glory."

"As always, *Lover* is an album Swift made for her fans. But it also feels like a record she made for herself, unburdened by external expectations and her own past," wrote the *A.V. Club. Variety* described it as "[an] exuberant album.... Event Pop where the sharing of emotions on a massive scale is the richest part of the blockbuster occasion."

Fun Fact: Taylor Swift was so affected by the movie *Something Great* that she kept dreaming about it. Ultimately, the song "Death by a Thousand Cuts" came out of the characters' strained dynamic. But that's not all. The writer/director of the film, Jenn Kaytin Robinson, was also inspired by Taylor, whose song "Clean" helped her through the very breakup that inspired the film's story. "I just wrote a song based on something she made, which she made while listening to something I made, which is the most meta thing that has ever happened to me," Taylor tweeted in 2019.

Release date: August 23, 2019

Track list:

1. I Forgot That You Existed
2. Cruel Summer
3. Lover
4. The Man
5. The Archer
6. I Think He Knows
7. Miss Americana & the Heartbreak Prince
8. Paper Rings
9. Cornelia Street
10. Death by a Thousand Cuts
11. London Boy
12. Soon You'll Get Better
13. False God
14. You Need to Calm Down
15. Afterglow
16. ME!
17. It's Nice to Have a Friend
18. Daylight

Folklore

COVID restrictions forced the cancellation of Taylor's Lover Fest world tour, along with just about everything else. But out of the lockdown came *Folklore*, which was produced remotely by longtime producer Jack Antonoff and new collaborator Aaron Dessner of the National. Musically, the folk-tinged record was new territory; it was also a departure lyrically—a concept album telling the story of three fictional teenagers caught in a love triangle. Taylor made clear to followers upon its release that this was not a typical Taylor Swift album, writing, "In isolation my imagination has run wild and this album is the result, a collection of songs and stories that flowed like a stream of consciousness." The visuals of the *Folklore* era are indelible: full cottagecore, a moss-covered fantasy.

Rolling Stone described a surprise album full of, well, surprises: "The most head-spinning, heartbreaking, emotionally ambitious songs of her life." *Paste* magazine called it "one of her best, most perfectly produced projects ever. In *Folklore*, [Taylor] wrote a quieter, more thought-provoking chapter in her constantly shape-shifting story."

Fun Fact: *Folklore* **is Taylor's longest-running album at Billboard's No. 1, holding the top spot for eight consecutive weeks. Bonus fun fact: it is also the album that has the most songs in the Eras Tour set!**

Release date: July 24, 2020

Track list:

1. The 1
2. Cardigan
3. The Last Great American Dynasty
4. Exile
5. My Tears Ricochet
6. Mirrorball
7. Seven
8. August
9. This Is Me Trying
10. Illicit Affairs
11. Invisible String
12. Mad Woman
13. Epiphany
14. Betty
15. Peace
16. Hoax

Evermore

The "sister record" to *Folklore*, *Evermore* appeared just five months later. Swift wrote, "To put it plainly, we just couldn't stop writing songs. To try and put it more poetically, it feels like we were standing on the edge of the folklorian woods and had a choice: to turn and go back or to travel further into the forest of this music. We chose to wander deeper in." *Spin* proclaimed it "the best work of her career," writing that with each album "she ascends further into the pantheon of songwriters who consistently deliver despite unimaginable expectations."

The *Evermore* era was a continuation of the world-building she achieved with *Folklore*, and indeed, many fans consider these two albums to comprise a single era. The world is one of mystery, fantasy, and intricately crafted lyrics.

Taylor's soft curls and darker locks indicated a more mature, confident persona than ever before, and her fashion reflected the sort of fantasy world that she created—woodsy, floral, and nubby, as if she were a forest nymph herself.

Fun Fact: *Evermore* **handed Taylor yet another Guinness World Record—this one for the shortest span between No. 1 albums for a female artist, with the album hitting No. 1 just 140 days after** *Folklore* **held the top spot.**

Release date: December 11, 2020

Track list:
1. Willow
2. Champagne Problems
3. Gold Rush
4. 'Tis the Damn Season
5. Tolerate It
6. No Body, No Crime
7. Happiness
8. Dorothea
9. Coney Island
10. Ivy
11. Cowboy Like Me
12. Long Story Short
13. Marjorie
14. Closure
15. Evermore

Midnights

Taylor describes *Midnights* as a concept album, a creative exercise pondering what keeps people up at night. But it is a deeply personal record too. Retreating from the fictional world of *Folklore* and *Evermore*, the songs on this record reflect the star's personal vulnerabilities laid bare, such as "Anti-Hero" and "Lavender Haze."

It seems repetitive to declare it her most successful release to date (again) and one that was widely critically acclaimed (again), but it was on both scores. It won Album of the Year at the 66th Annual Grammy Awards in 2024, Taylor's fourth such award. As *PopMatters* wrote in its 2022 review of *Midnights*, "It allows Swift to do what she has always wanted: make an album for its own sake that is received primarily as a work of art instead of a commercial entity or tabloid fodder. Indeed, on *Midnights* she is more self-assured than ever—letting more go, taking more chances, and making no apologies."

The *Midnights* era reflected the restless, late-night energy of its concept. The low-key 1970s glamour of the looks, such as those seen in the video for "Anti-Hero," give a spooky Laurel Canyon vibe.

Release date: October 21, 2022

Track list:

1. Lavender Haze
2. Maroon
3. Anti-Hero
4. Snow on the Beach
5. You're on Your Own, Kid
6. Midnight Rain
7. Question...?
8. Vigilante Shit
9. Bejeweled
10. Labyrinth
11. Karma
12. Sweet Nothing
13. Mastermind

Fun Fact: The title for "Lavender Haze" was inspired by a line of dialogue in the TV series *Mad Men.*

The Tortured Poets Department

If *Reputation*'s black-and-white imagery was confrontational, the vibe of *The Tortured Poets Department*'s black-and-white photography is quiet and intimate. For an artist known for her confessional writing style, *TTPD* may indeed be her most personal album yet.

The wide-ranging album pulls influences from a vast range of inspirations and is chock full of references. Where else could you find a record that nods to early American cinema, Biblical scholarship, little-known political documents, the poetry of Dylan Thomas, the Chelsea Hotel in the 1960s, and even Charlie Puth. It also features a pair of guest artists with serious star power: Post Malone and Florence Welch of Florence and the Machine.

It's too early to tell everything this era will be remembered for, but out of the gate the reaction to the music has been overwhelmingly positive. *Rolling Stone* called it an "instant classic" and *People* wrote that Taylor "bares her soul and settles scores on her prolific new album."

Fun Fact: *TTPD* sold 1.4 million copies on just its first *day* of release, Taylor's highest mark yet and one of the biggest of all time.

Release date: April 19, 2024

Track list:
1. Fortnight
2. The Tortured Poets Department
3. My Boy Only Breaks His Favorite Toys
4. Down Bad
5. So Long, London
6. But Daddy I Love Him
7. Fresh Out of the Slammer
8. Florida!!!
9. Guilty As Sin?
10. Who's Afraid of Little Old Me?
11. I Can Fix Him (No Really I Can)
12. Loml
13. I Can Do It with a Broken Heart
14. The Smallest Man Who Ever Lived
15. The Alchemy
16. Clara Bow

The Tortured Poets Department: The Anthology

And then, as Taylor put it to Swifties in the wee hours of *TTPD*'s release date, "a 2 a.m. surprise": she was releasing an expanded edition featuring an entire album's worth of extra music. *The Tortured Poets Department: The Anthology* includes all four previously announced bonus tracks from the original's deluxe edition—"The Manuscript," "The Black Dog," "The Albatross," and "The Bolter"—plus an additional eleven singles. Astute listeners will recognize many of the subjects featured on the album; they are far from obscured. (Look, for example, at the capitalization of "thanK you aIMee" or the football-tinged lyrics of "The Anthology" and "So High School.")

As Taylor wrote upon its release, "This writer is of the firm belief that our tears become holy in the form of ink on a page. Once we have spoken our saddest story, we can be free of it. And then all that's left behind is the tortured poetry." Taylor, more than ever, seems ready to close the book on all the bad blood and heartaches of the past. What will the next era bring?

Fun Fact: *The Anthology* **features five songs written solely by Taylor ("The Black Dog," "The Manuscript," "My Boy Only Breaks His Favorite Toys," "Who's Afraid of Little Old Me?" and "Peter"), the most since** *Red.*

Release date: April 19, 2024

Additional tracks:

17. The Black Dog
18. imgonnagetyouback
19. The Albatross
20. Chloe or Sam or Sophia or Marcus
21. How Did It End?
22. So High School
23. I Hate It Here
24. thanK you aIMee
25. I Look in People's Windows
26. The Prophecy
27. Cassandra
28. Peter
29. The Bolter
30. Robin
31. The Manuscript

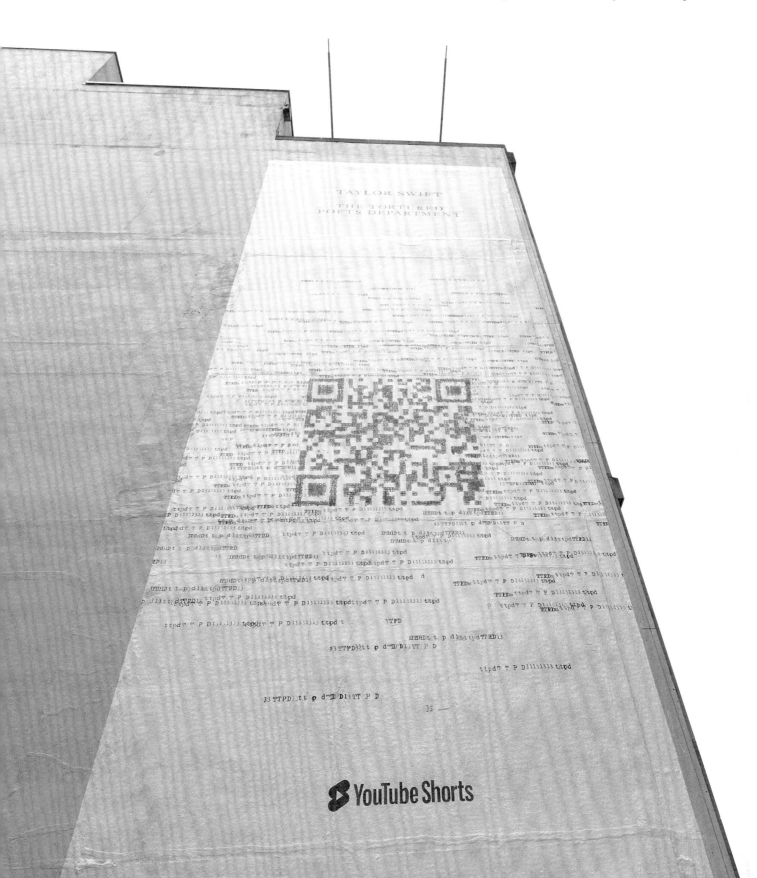

The marketing campaign for *The Tortured Poets Department* featured unique elements, like this cryptic code that appeared overnight on a building in Chicago.

chapter 4

SPEAK NOW

In the music industry, it's hard to imagine a bigger advocate for other artists than Taylor Swift. Given her influence, she's been able to press for industry-wide change in a way that most other artists could not.

When the digital age upended the music business, with artists getting paid a fraction of a penny for their work from streaming sites hiding behind opaque algorithms, Taylor wrote an op-ed in the *Wall Street Journal* that read in part, "Music is art, and art is important and rare. Important, rare things are valuable. Valuable things should be paid for. It's my opinion that music should not be free."

Then she pulled her entire catalog of music from Spotify, full stop. "I'm not willing to contribute my life's work to an experiment that I don't feel fairly compensates the writers, producers, artists, and creators of this music," she told Yahoo. Her moves against unfair streaming practices have had some effect. Her parent company, Universal (one of three major US labels), now allows all of their artists to opt out of streaming in their albums' first two weeks, giving them a chance to earn more through physical album sales.

Taylor also uplifts artists in other ways, promoting them whenever and however she can. A voracious consumer of music, Taylor is an unabashed fan who has brought on scores of tourmates whom she genuinely admires, from Haim to Phoebe Bridgers to Camila Cabello. It's important to Taylor that she lifts up other women around her, describing her fellow artists as a sorority of sorts.

65,000

Observers call it the Taylor Swift Effect, and it describes the artist's ability to impact everything from social media trends to nationwide economies. In 2022, just twenty-four hours after urging followers on social media to get out the vote, Vote.org reported a massive spike in new voter registrations, with more than sixty-five thousand new registrants in a single day.

Taylor doesn't get
mad, she gets GLAAD.

First Lady Michelle Obama presents Taylor with the Big Help Award, in recognition of the artist's charity work, in 2012.

"Other women who are killing it should motivate you, thrill you, challenge you, and inspire you," she said to *Time* in 2014. But it's not just the ladies; Taylor brought the likes of Ed Sheeran, Shawn Mendes, and Vance Joy, among others, on the road when their careers were in their infancy.

Taylor has also always been a staunch self-advocate, railing against sexism in the industry and standing firm when it counted. Songs such as "The Man" and "Miss Americana & the Heartbreak Prince" deal with the gender double standard pointedly, but it's woven into the fabric of *all* of her music. She's also been quick to call out journalists more interested in her love life than her music, or who ask when she's going to have children or which ex a song is about. "People...say, 'Oh, you know, like, she just writes songs about her ex-boyfriends.' And I think frankly that's a very sexist angle to take. No one says that about Ed Sheeran. No one says that about Bruno Mars. They're all writing songs about their exes, their current girlfriends, their love life, and no one raises the red flag there," Taylor told 2DayFM.

She's on a quest to dismantle the idea that *feminism* is a dirty word. "Misogyny is ingrained in people from the time they are born," Taylor told *Maxim* in December 2015. "So, to me, feminism is probably the most important movement that you could embrace, because it's just basically another word for equality. A man writing about his feelings from a vulnerable place is brave; a woman writing about her feelings from a vulnerable place is oversharing or whining."

After years of "being polite at all costs," as she describes it, and keeping out of politics, Taylor decided she could no longer keep silent. The documentary *Miss Americana* shines a dramatic light on Taylor as she stood at that precipice, eager to speak her mind but knowing there was no turning back once she did. Members of her inner circle, including her own father, urged her not to do it, fearing she'd slash her fan base in half if she took a political stance. She went with her conscience, excoriating Tennessee senator Marsha Blackburn for her voting record and mistreatment of marginalized people.

"Everyone should be able to live out their love story without fear of discrimination."

—Taylor, upon accepting an Attitude Icon Award for her LGBTQ+ advocacy work

Taylor is a strong ally for the LGBTQ+ community, tackling gay rights and marriage equality head-on in songs like "You Need to Calm Down." "Who you love and how you identify shouldn't put you in danger, leave you vulnerable or hold you back in life," she tweeted pointedly.

She publicly petitioned for the Equality Act, starting a petition on Change.org that netted more than eight hundred thousand signatures, eight times more than required for it to make its way to Congress for consideration. "I didn't realize until recently that I could advocate for a community that I'm not a part of," she told *Vogue*. The Equality Act, which provides protections against discrimination on the basis of sexual orientation and gender, was signed into law by President Joe Biden in 2022.

If promoting equal rights for everyone courts more controversy for Taylor, she's made peace with it. She's taken lumps before, and she's still standing. "Obviously anytime you're standing up for or against anything, you're never going to receive unanimous praise," she told *Variety* in 2020. "But that's what forces you to be brave. And that's what's different about the way I live my life now."

Taylor has a long history of supporting female artists. Here she is performing with friends and fellow musicians Haim on tour in 2023.

Taylor performs "You Need to Calm Down" at the 2019 VMAs.

She's argued fiercely against gun violence, police brutality, the erosion of reproductive freedom, and bigotry in all its forms. Having found her voice, she continues to encourage her supporters to be full-throated in using their own.

Going into the next election cycle, journalists speculate whether Swifties could tip the scales there. Some pundits, terrified by her potential influence, have even gone so far as to suggest that Swift herself is a spy whose mission is to tilt the election. That's ludicrous, of course, but proof positive that Swifties are indeed a voting bloc to be reckoned with.

But so far in 2024, Taylor has not endorsed a single political candidate, simply urging her voters to "Vote the people who most represent YOU into power," which she posted in an Instagram Story to her 242 million followers on the day of the Super Tuesday primaries.

Whether or not her influence determines voting outcomes is still subject to debate, but there's no denying that she's changed the hearts and minds of many who have listened to her music and heard her words. And for Taylor, that's exactly the legacy she wants to have. ★

"I wanna love glitter
and also stand up
for the double standards
that exist in our society.
I wanna wear pink
and tell you how
I feel about politics,
and I don't think that
those things have to
cancel each other out."

chapter 5

BEJEWELED

Striking gold at the Grammys in 2016.

Like any artist, Taylor surrounds herself with a massive team of talented people who help guide her career. Having said that, there is not one facet of Taylor's career in which she is not involved. She has been responsible for blazing a trail all her own, and her vision and determination have taken her to the pinnacle of success where she reigns today.

She's gotten there on her own terms, and based on her entirely unique merits. "Swift is an oddball," *New York* writes. "There is no real historical precedent for her. Her path to stardom has defied the established patterns; she falls between genres, eras, demographics, paradigms, and trends.... Swift's influence has reverberated through popular music, yet she remains *sui generis*, a genre of one."

A list of Taylor's superlatives would fill this entire book and then some—and is ever growing. So too are the awards she's garnered so far over the span of her incredible career. The following is a rundown of some of the major accolades she's received so far:

4

With *Midnights*, Taylor became the only artist to win Album of the Year for a fourth time. She previously won the Grammys' highest honor for *Fearless* (2009), *1989* (2015), and *Folklore* (2020).

Grammy Awards: Taylor has fifty-two nominations and fourteen wins, including four Album of the Year awards and seven Song of the Year nominations.

MTV Video Music Awards: Taylor has forty-two nominations and twenty-three wins, including wins for Video of the Year for "You Belong with Me," "Bad Blood," and "Anti-Hero," and Best Longform Video for "All Too Well (10 Minute Version)." In 2023 she tied the record for most VMAs won in a single night, netting nine Moonmen.

American Music Awards: Taylor is the most awarded artist of all time at the AMAs, with forty wins, including seven Artist of the Year honors.

Billboard Music Awards: Taylor has thirty-nine BBMAs, tying Drake for most wins in BBMA history, and has been nominated a whopping ninety times!

TAYLOR SWIFT

Country Music Association Awards: While Taylor may not be considered a country artist anymore, she's still getting attention from the Country Music Association. She nabbed a 2022 nomination for a rerecorded track from *Red* that she released on *Red (Taylor's Version)*, featuring Chris Stapleton. Altogether Taylor has ten CMAs, the most prestigious honor in country music.

Billboard named Taylor their first-ever Woman of the Decade in 2019, calling her "one of the most accomplished artists of all time." Announcing her honor, *Billboard* wrote, "Swift has landed countless professional achievements.... The singer-songwriter is also being honored for her commitment to protecting creative rights, music education, literacy programs, cancer research, disaster relief, and the Time's Up initiative." And in 2022, Taylor was named Songwriter-Artist of the Decade by the Nashville Songwriters Association and the Artist of the Decade by the American Music Awards.

She's directed thirteen of her own music videos, including some of her most unforgettable: "ME!," "Anti-Hero," "Karma," and the hilarious "The Man," in which Taylor, in drag, answers her own musical question, experiencing what it would feel like to walk the world as a man.

Accepting Album of the Year honors with *Midnights* collaborators (left to right) Phoebe Bridgers, Julien Baker, and Lucy Dacus.

Perhaps the most ambitious of all, Taylor went behind the camera to direct the film that accompanies the ten-minute version of "All Too Well," a longtime fan favorite from *Red* that was never released as a single. The short film premiered at the prestigious Tribeca Festival in 2022. *NME* wrote that the film "highlights the emotional power of [Swift's] unrivalled storytelling. That's in part thanks to some electric performances from *Stranger Things'* Sadie Sink and [*The*] *Maze Runner*'s Dylan O'Brien, but it would be nothing without the vulnerable creativity of the songwriter herself, who also wrote the story for the short."

The overwhelming response to the short film may have Taylor setting her sights even higher. "It would be so fantastic to write and direct...a feature," Taylor told *Variety* in 2022. "I don't see it being bigger, in terms of scale. I loved making a film that was so intimate." To be sure, intimacy is Taylor's brand.

In front of the lens, she's even dabbled in acting, guest-starring on TV shows *CSI* and *The New Girl* and appearing in Hollywood movies including the ensemble rom-com *Valentine's Day*, *The Giver*, and most recently David O. Russell's *Amsterdam*. She also delivered purr-fection in the screen adaptation of

Oh My Guinness!

As of this writing, Taylor Swift owns a staggering 118 Guinness World Records. According to the institution, which is *the* authority on superlatives, she owns a slew of top marks in revenues, streaming, touring, chart history, and social media engagement, just to name a few. In 2023 she broke several records, including most cumulative weeks at No. 1 on the Billboard 200 (63), highest-grossing concert tour (still ongoing), most simultaneous albums on the Billboard 200 chart for a living artist (10), most No. 1 albums (10), most single chart entries for a female artist (212), most top 10 debuts for a female artist (31), most simultaneous new entries on the Billboard Hot 100 by a female artist (26), and most monthly listeners on Spotify for a female artist (100 million). And with the release of *The Tortured Poets Department* in 2024, she's broken many of her own records all over again.

Director Swift poses with stars Dylan O'Brien and Sadie Sink at the premiere of *All Too Well*.

Taylor accepts Woman of the Decade honors from Billboard in 2019.

Andrew Lloyd Weber's beloved musical *Cats*, performing "Macavity the Mystery Cat" as character Bombalurina.

The success of Taylor's Eras Tour documentary was hailed by some as single-handedly reviving the flagging movie theater industry. The movie shattered ticket marks for a concert film and considerably boosted overall box office numbers, earning nearly $180 million domestically and more than $250 million worldwide during its theatrical release. Her exclusive deal with AMC Theaters also created a road map for artists to follow in this brave new (and segmented) world of media.

Is there anything Taylor can't do? She's focused, thoughtful, and determined to give her best effort, so whatever she tries her hand at next, odds are she'll succeed. ★

"A lot of people have been the biggest. Not a lot of people have been the biggest and the best, but she is."

—Jack Antonoff

Golden Girl

With so many awards, accolades, and accomplishments, it can be hard to keep them all straight. Okay, Swifties, it's your turn. Do you know a thing about Taylor's bling? Find out by taking the quiz below. (Answers appear on page 126.)

1. **How old was Taylor when she won her first Grammy?**
   a. sixteen
   b. eighteen
   c. twenty
   d. twenty-two

2. **Taylor is the most awarded artist of all time at the American Music Awards. Which of her albums won the most AMAs?**

3. **What is the name of the song for which Taylor was nominated for a 2022 Country Music Association Award?**

4. **Which Taylor song was nominated for an Academy Award?**

5. **How many times has Taylor been nominated for a Golden Globe Award?**

6. **Which award was Taylor accepting when she was famously interrupted onstage by Kanye West?**

7. **Taylor has directed lots of her own music videos. Which one was the first to net her a Grammy for direction?**

8. **Which group did *not* nominate Taylor for Best New Artist (or equivalent) for her debut?**
   a. Grammys
   b. Academy of Country Music
   c. Nickelodeon Kids' Choice Awards
   d. MTV Video Music Awards

9. **Which organization awarded Taylor with the Vanguard Award for her work as an ally with the LGBTQ+ community?**

10. **Which of the following has not named Taylor Swift a Songwriter/Artist of the Decade?**
    a. Billboard Music Awards
    b. American Music Awards
    c. Nashville Songwriter Awards
    d. iHeartRadio Music Awards

Hoisting an armful of awards at the 2013 BBMAs.

chapter 6

NEW
ROMANTICS

As the calendar year turned from 2023 to 2024, there was no bigger news story than Taylor and Travis. Maybe people were looking for a little good news among the otherwise bleak headlines. Or maybe they wanted a little peek into the lives of two mega-celebrities. Whatever the reason, the romance between Kansas City Chiefs tight end Travis Kelce and Taylor Swift seemed to capture the whole world's attention. However unlikely it is that the world's most successful recording artist would become an NFL WAG (short for "wives and girlfriends"), here we were. Suddenly, the superstar who couldn't get any bigger...did.

It all started back in July 2023, when Taylor's Eras Tour rolled through Kansas City. Kelce attended the concert but came away disappointed when he wasn't able to connect with Taylor directly. That foiled Kelce's plan, which was to slip the singer a friendship bracelet he'd brought with his phone number on it. Recounting the story to his brother, Jason, on their *New Heights* podcast, he described being bummed out by his failed grand gesture: "I was

7

According to Nielsen, NFL games saw a 7 percent increase in viewership during the 2023 season— and a 50+ percent increase among females aged twelve to seventeen.

disappointed that she doesn't talk before or after the shows because she has to save her voice for the forty-four songs that she sings," he said. "So I was a little [hurt] I didn't get to hand her one of the bracelets I made for her."

It wasn't long before Taylor got wind of the plot. "Travis very adorably put me on blast on his podcast, which I thought was metal as hell," she recalled to *Time* in December 2023. "We started hanging out right after that. So we actually had a significant amount of time that no one knew [about], which I'm grateful for, because we got to get to know each other."

Rumors began swirling about the couple's dating status as August turned to September, but the two stars remained tight-lipped about their connection, downplaying reports of a romantic relationship. Kelce, appearing on *The Pat McAfee Show* on September 21, coyly said, "I threw the ball in her court.... I told her, 'I've seen you rock the stage in Arrowhead; you might have to come see me rock the stage at Arrowhead and see which one's a little

Travis reportedly spent more than $1 million to level up his wardrobe once he began dating Taylor.

more lit, so we'll see what happens in the near future."

Three days later, Taylor was in box seats at Arrowhead Stadium, decked out in full Chiefs regalia and seated beside Kelce's mom, Donna Kelce, as Kansas City took on the Chicago Bears. (It was months later when it was ultimately revealed the couple had already been privately dating for several weeks at that point.) With one public appearance, what was once speculation became a full-blown media frenzy, as photographers scrambled to get shots of the two and writers scrambled for tiny details to report on—where they went, what they did, and even what they called each other.

The couple, no strangers to media attention, took it in stride. "When you say a relationship is public, that means I'm going to see him do what he loves," Taylor told *Time*. "We're showing up for each other. Other people are there, and we don't care. The opposite of that is you have to go to an extreme amount of

That's a Dynamite Gift

Travis commissioned his-and-hers custom tennis bracelets from Pennsylvania jeweler Wove. The customizable bracelets are crafted from 14 karat yellow gold and feature three gold beads with pavé diamonds spelling out T-N-T. Taylor's version, estimated at more than $6,000, features nearly five carats of diamonds. Travis's is a little larger; his band has almost ten carats in diamonds. And in a full-circle moment, the items are part of a line from A-list athlete and golfer Michelle

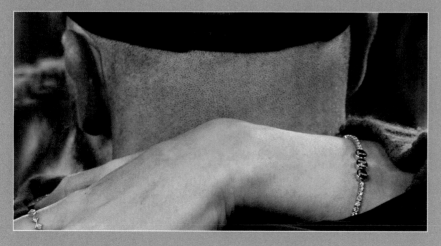

Wie West, who worked with the jeweler to create a customizable, luxury version of the friendship bracelets made ubiquitous by—you guessed it—Taylor Swift and the Swifties themselves.

The Taylor Swift Effect boosted Super Bowl viewership; the game saw a record-high 123.4 million viewers.

The couple attended Coachella to support pals Lana Del Rey and Jack Antonoff of Bleachers, both of whom played the festival.

"I would say that Travis Kelce has had a lot of big catches in his career. This would be the biggest."

—NFL head coach Bill Belichick to WEEI Radio

effort to make sure no one knows that you're seeing someone. And we're just proud of each other."

An entire nation was instantly captivated. *Billboard* described Kelce as "a well-liked, unproblematic figure, a Super Bowl–winning superstar as an athlete with enough of a Q rating as a celebrity to host *SNL*" and stated that his love match with Taylor "was universally accessible, and found near-100% public approval. You didn't need deep grounding in Swift Lore to understand the relationship, because it just felt right: the All-American athlete dating the All-American pop star."

Not only did their relationship capture the attention of people everywhere, but it translated into big business for the NFL and beyond. The Kelce brothers' podcast, *New Heights*, skyrocketed to the top of Apple's streaming charts. Viewership for the NFL increased dramatically—no small thing considering NFL football is

consistently the top television ratings-getter among all programming—and the league boasted its highest female viewership in decades. Sales for Pro Bowler Kelce's jerseys spiked by 400 percent. Stadiums were packed with young fans hoping to get a glimpse of Swift and carrying signs that read "Go Taylor's Boyfriend" and "Where's Taylor?" Apex Marketing Group, an independent researcher, reported that Taylor Swift's influence added more than $330 million to the Chiefs' brand value.

The impact their relationship has had on the game is not lost on the league. "Having the 'Taylor Swift Effect'… creates a buzz, it creates another group of young fans—particularly young women—that are interested in seeing: *Why is she going to this game?*" said NFL commissioner Roger Goodell.

Taylor's historic night at the 2024 Grammys, just a week before Super Bowl LVIII (she won a history-making fourth Album of the Year award), added one last bit of inspiration for Kelce. He told media before the game, "She's unbelievable. She's rewriting the history books herself, and I told her I'd have to hold up my end of the bargain and come home with some hardware too."

True to his word, Kelce and the Kansas City Chiefs took home the Vince Lombardi Trophy, cementing a banner year for both Travis and Taylor—two entertainers at the absolute top of their respective games.

As of press time, Taylor and Travis are still going strong. They've been spotted by paparazzi across the globe in places as far-flung as Singapore, Australia, and the Bahamas. And in March 2024 Travis added fuel to swirling engagement rumors while making a comment on *New Heights* about starting a family someday. With Taylor on hiatus from tour in the spring of 2024 and Kelce in the NFL off-season, the pair made Los Angeles home while Travis pursued Hollywood opportunities including hosting duties on *Are You Smarter Than a Celebrity?* and a role in Ryan Murphy's new horror series, *Grotesquerie*.

The next chapter of the pair's romance is yet to be written, but for now, TNT is still blowing up. "I'm the happiest I've ever been," Kelce told *People* in April 2024. "I'm oozing life right now." ★

Taylor's first visit to Chiefs Kingdom, in September 2023. She watched the game alongside Mama Kelce.

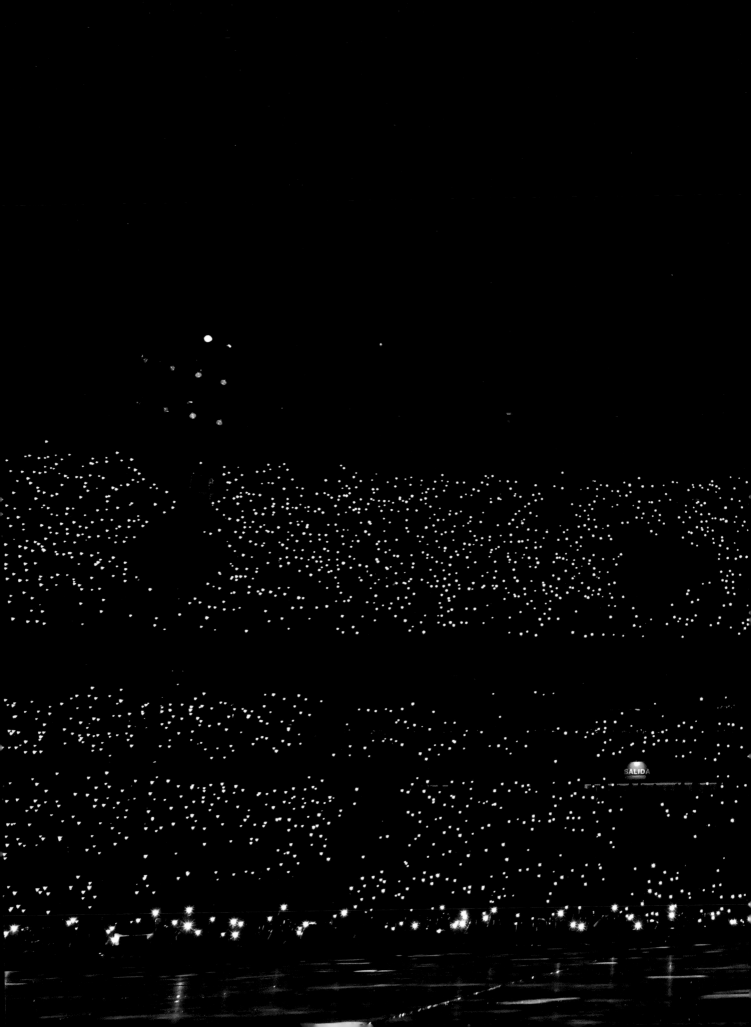

chapter 7

SPARKS FLY

Taylor performs a song from *Evermore* during the Eras Tour in July 2023.

Taylor hasn't been on tour since her 2018 Reputation Tour. (Lover Fest tour, in support of *Lover*, was scuttled by the lockdowns in 2020.) Given that, when her Eras Tour was first announced—billed by Taylor as "a journey through the musical eras of my career (past and present!)"—it was reasonable to expect there'd be excitement. What most people didn't expect, however, was that it would break the internet.

Demand for presale tickets was so high that Ticketmaster's website completely shut down due to unprecedented traffic, leaving devastated Swifties out in the cold. Pre-verified ticket buyers waited hours in virtual waiting rooms for their guaranteed tickets before being told they were out of luck. What's more, the vendor announced that general sales for the Eras Tour were canceled due to lack of inventory. The fiasco made national headlines and took weeks to sort out. It even drew the ire of lawmakers in Congress, who railed against the ticket broker's monopoly.

For those lucky enough to get a ticket—and that amounts to millions of fans around the world—the Eras Tour delivers. The show packs in forty-four songs (including surprise selections that vary from city to city) taken from every one of Taylor's first ten albums, from *Taylor Swift* to *Midnights*, into a marathon three-and-a-half-hour extravaganza. It includes giant set pieces, multiple wardrobe changes, pyrotechnics, special effects, and moss—lots and lots of moss. There's a performance where Taylor appears to dive into the stage and swim. There's another where she croons from atop a fairy-tale cottage. And then there's the three-story Lover House, a giant Easter egg–filled set piece with hidden meanings galore.

2.3

Fans at a 2023 show in Seattle were *shook*. They rocked the stadium so much that the seismic activity registered a 2.3 on the Richter scale.

The scope and ambition in the tour is remarkable. In terms of live tours, it's difficult to find anything to compare it to, period. "I knew this tour was harder than anything I'd ever done before by a long shot," Swift told *Time* in 2023.

Each era has its own act within the overall show, and features its own signature costumes, created by some of the most distinguished fashion houses in the world. Versace created the jewel-encrusted bodysuits Taylor wears during her *Lover* set, as well as the power blazers worn during "The Man." Roberto Cavalli brought his fringe game for the swingy *Fearless* dresses, and also made the unmistakable serpent bodysuit for *Reputation*. Looks for *Evermore* were done by Etro. Couturier Nicole + Felicia created multiple gowns, including the dreamy "Enchanted" dress made from tiers upon tiers of lavender tulle. Other heavy hitters, including Elie Saab, Zuhair Murad,

Alberta Ferretti, and Oscar de la Renta, contributed looks. And famed shoe designer Christian Louboutin (known for his signature red-soled creations) custom-designed most of the footwear worn onstage, including multiple pairs of sparkly boots.

Each show features two surprise songs chosen for the specific location, along with surprise guests at every stop—everyone from Ice Spice and Phoebe Bridgers to Aaron Dessner and even Taylor Lautner has popped in.

Tragedy Strikes

On November 17, 2023, the unthinkable happened: a young concertgoer named Ana Clara Benevides Machado passed out while attending the Eras Tour in Rio de Janeiro, and died hours later from cardiopulmonary arrest due to heat exhaustion and dehydration. She was just twenty-three years old. At the time of the concert, Brazil was in the midst of an intense heat wave, with temperatures climbing to 105 degrees Fahrenheit. Stadium rules did not allow fans to bring their own water bottles inside the venue. There was water inside, but getting it proved onerous, leading many to experience heat exhaustion. It was so bad, in fact, that Swift herself called on stadium staff for water to be distributed to fans at multiple times during her performance.

Upon hearing the awful news hours later, a stunned Taylor wrote, "I can't believe I'm writing these words, but it is with a shattered heart that I say we lost a fan earlier tonight.... I can't even tell you how devastated I am by this. There's very little information I have other than the fact that she was so incredibly beautiful and far too young." Weeks later, Taylor invited Benavides's family to her show in São Paulo, where she sang "Bigger Than the Whole Sky" in Ana's honor.

Onstage in São Paulo, Brazil, on the South American leg of the Eras Tour.

She played three and a half hours in a downpour at a March 2023 gig in Foxborough, Massachusetts.

By December 2023, with the tour only partially completed, it became the highest-grossing live tour of all time with $1 billion in ticket revenue, eclipsing Elton John's five-year-long farewell tour. By the time the Eras Tour wraps in late 2024, it is expected to have doubled that mark, earning more than $2 billion in its staggering run.

"Taylor Swift is an economic genius," said Alan Krueger, former chairman of the Council of Economic Advisers under Obama and author of *Rockonomics*. The book explains the shift in the music industry. Years ago, record sales were the primary income for musicians. But as labels gobbled up more and more of that revenue share for themselves, touring became the primary moneymaker for artists.

No one has harnessed the power of touring quite like Taylor. As of this writing, the Eras Tour will cross 5 continents with 152 dates spanning 18 countries. And with this record-setting achievement, it's clear that Taylor is the rare global superstar who can fill stadiums seemingly anywhere she goes.

Writing to fans on social media in 2023, she called the Eras Tour "the most meaningful, electric experience of my life so far." ★

The Eras Tour: By the Numbers

152: The number of concerts performed on the Eras Tour once the tour concludes in late 2024.

5: The number of continents visited: North America, South America, Europe, Asia, and Australia.

$238: The average ticket price per concertgoer on the Eras Tour.

$1,637: The average resale price for an Eras ticket, according to SeatGeek.

72,000: The average number of people in attendance per concert.

3½: The length of an Eras Tour concert, in hours.

44: The number of songs performed each night...

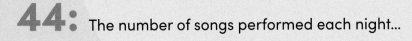

17: ...spanning seventeen years in Taylor's career.

10: The number of acts in each concert.

16: The number of costume changes made by Taylor during an Eras Tour performance.

4.3 million: The number of tickets sold for the Eras Tour, according to Pollstar.

$17.3 million: The estimated amount in ticket sales earned per show on the Eras Tour.

$200 million: The estimated amount earned from merchandise sales on the Eras Tour once it wraps.

16: The number of backup dancers who appear onstage.

$2.17 billion: The total estimated amount expected to be earned by the Eras Tour by the time it ends its 152-date run.

chapter 8
OUR SONG

A NEW ERA

Sometimes it feels like there's not a lot people can agree on these days. But there's one thing that seems assured: everybody likes Taylor Swift. According to a recent survey conducted by Morning Consult, more than half of Americans consider themselves fans of the artist, with 16 percent describing themselves as "avid fans." Surprisingly, fewer than half of those avid fans are millennials, followed by baby boomers (23%), Gen Xers (21%), and Gen Z and younger (11%). What's more, her fan base is almost evenly split by gender (52% female and 48% male).

It's a testament to Taylor that she can draw such an eclectic fan base across a wide spectrum of ages. Certainly it speaks volumes about the universality of her music. But the music is just one of many ways in which she connects with Swifties. She's intentional and resolute in engaging with her fans however she can, and never misses an opportunity to express her gratitude for Swifties. She calls them "the most generous, thoughtful, loving fans on the planet," saying at the end of the *Eras Tour* movie, "This is all because of you and for you."

Taylor actively engages on social media (that includes more than 283 million followers on Instagram, 95M on X, 57M on YouTube, and 25M on TikTok), where she regularly communicates with fans. What's more, while some of social media's top dogs have seen relatively flat numbers over the past few years, Taylor's numbers keep climbing steadily. It's on her channels that she makes major announcements, and teases hints and snippets about forthcoming music.

She shines a light on her process, whether it's giving fans access to behind-the-scenes production (songwriting, studio time, music video production) or sharing the inspirations behind the music.

And Taylor goes out of her way to meet with fans, whether it's at publicity events, tour stops, or other venues. Her Secret Sessions are epic too. In celebration of a new album, she has hosted groups of Swifties at her homes to preview the music before its release. It's a fan experience like none other. They can take pictures with the singer and are treated to home-baked goods made by Taylor herself. Swifties have even snapped photos holding her Grammys or even her cats!

True to her own personality, Taylor emphasizes bringing the fun. She methodically includes Easter eggs for fans interspersed in her lyrics, music videos, and social media posts. It's a practice she's done since her very first album, burying hidden messages in her liner notes, interspersing stray capital letters in her song lyrics.

"When I was fifteen and putting together my first album...I decided to encode the lyrics with hidden messages using capital letters. That's how it started, and my fans and I have since descended into color coding, numerology, word searches, elaborate hints, and Easter eggs," she told the *Washington Post*. "It's really about turning new music into an event for my fans and trying to entertain them in playful, mischievous, clever ways. As long as they still find it fun and exciting, I'll keep doing it."

The practice has turned Swifties into amateur cryptologists, speculating about songs' inspirations and spinning wild theories about music and what might be coming next. (Unsurprisingly, Taylor often chimes in on social media to confirm or deny some of those theories.) Astute viewers and listeners are quick to point out the details buried in music videos, or oblique references woven into her lyrics. The enthusiasm for the "hunt" can be seen most recently in the slow rollout of *The Tortured Poets Department*. Fans have seen hidden meanings in everything from the song titles to the release date to the publicity images. The last of which, some say, are mirror images of the photographs from

Midnights, leading fans to speculate that this is its sister album, like *Midnights* in the Upside Down à la *Stranger Things*. (And jeez, *Stranger Things* star Sadie Sink was the leading lady in the "All Too Well" film—connections everywhere!)

As a collective, the Swifties are a force to be reckoned with. Through sheer force of will, they have helped elevate Taylor to the superstardom she enjoys today. As they have proved time and again, they're incredibly disciplined, organized, and enthusiastic about every Swiftian milestone, whether it's a new single, album, or (perhaps especially) tour.

"Because the Swifties feel so seen by Swift—both personally and through her music—they put their full power behind the singer," wrote *American Songwriter*. "The Swifties won't let Swift lose at anything she does. It's a symbiotic relationship that has yet to be replicated in the music industry."

They're also ardently loyal to one another. They are a community unto themselves, spreading love, messages of support, and shared joy in every missive. Swifties do not tolerate trolls or negativity. They're there for each other. Stories about Swifties helping other Swifties populate the media: whether it's sending messages of hope to a Swiftie suffering from illness, stepping in with financial assists for Swifties when tragedy strikes, or assembling to support causes near and dear to them, they are a loyal and dedicated network of global citizens. As BeMe Health

wrote, "Being a Swiftie is not just about enjoying great music; it's about building friendships, embracing your emotions, and nurturing your mental well-being."

Nowhere is this spirit of friendship more apparent than on tour. Swifties around

Taylor gives a hat to a young fan at each Eras show.

Swifties flocked to the NFL, boosting already-enormous league revenues.

the world have gathered for the Eras Tour en masse. Wearing sleeves of friendship bracelets, many with "13" written on their hands—a nod to Taylor's lucky number and *Red*-era practice, when the singer would perform with "13" written on her own hand—they have all come together dressed up in styles from their favorite era.

So far cities on the Eras Tour have been overtaken by pure, unbridled joy—along with the power of the almighty dollar. Local economies—particularly in the food, hospitality, and transportation sectors—have spiked massively around each Eras Tour date. The impact is roughly on par with the boost a city sees from the most coveted of engagements: the Super Bowl. All told, economists suggest that Swifties will add more than $5 billion to local economies across the Era Tour's U.S. locations. What's more, the U.S. Travel Association reports that that number might be closer to $10 billion when taking into account the indirect spending of those who do not attend the concert itself but spent around the event.

The Swifties' superpowers lie not just in their numbers but in their enthusiasm. They're a powerful force for good who show up for Taylor, and for each other. ★

Male and female, young and old, *everyone* comes dressed to impress at a Taylor Swift concert.

Swifties Speak

Taylor's fans are tried and true. Whether it's lining up for a new album release, engaging online, or showing up in person to the Eras Tour, Swifties make their voices heard! Below are just a few fans showing the love.

"Taylor Swift and her music have helped me through a lot. I am so thankful that she is here to help and support me and her other fans."—Izzie Bahr, age 11

"[Taylor is] one of the greatest songwriters of our generation."—Adele

"I like that she writes her own songs. Not a lot of pop stars do that. And I like how supportive she is of other singers! At the Grammys she was singing along, dancing, and cheering for all the performers."—Marlowe S., age 10

"I'm just a sucker for a gal who is good with words, and she is the best with them."—Greta Gerwig

"Taylor Swift's music is such a gift to the world, and the way she fosters community is so brilliant." —John Green, author of *The Fault in Our Stars*

"I'm totally into Taylor Swift. I think she has super-clever lyrics, and I love that she writes her own music. Some of the themes she writes about are stuff I wish was there for me when I was in high school, and I'm so happy she really cares about her female fans."—Kathleen Hanna (Bikini Kill)

"Taylor makes the job of creating music for millions of people look easy."—Shawn Mendes

"Deepest gratitude to @taylorswift for your poetry and wisdom. You inspire us and connect us to our #delicate tenderness, joy, hope and strength—and most of all, our wish to live and love courageously."—Mariska Hargitay (*Law & Order: SVU*)

She's been honored time and again for her songwriting, including here, in 2010 as Songwriter of the Year at the 2010 BMI Country Awards.

Star Search

Swifties know *all too well* that her albums are *bejeweled* with a *labyrinth* of Easter eggs and hidden messages in practically every *blank space*—that's just her *style*. The challenge is on! Can you find the thirteen song titles hidden in this word search? (Need a hint? See the word bank on page 126.)

S	I	F	G	E	V	J	W	A	T	D	I	G	C	N	E	N	I	A	L
I	M	X	Q	T	Y	D	L	A	R	A	T	J	U	N	O	P	N	M	V
S	H	A	K	E	I	T	O	F	F	M	I	Z	C	E	T	H	U	K	L
A	D	E	E	C	B	N	M	H	N	U	O	H	S	S	E	Q	R	T	O
N	R	Y	I	R	O	D	L	E	X	C	A	R	D	I	G	A	N	T	P
G	H	T	Y	N	D	E	R	E	T	N	C	C	U	A	R	W	U	J	O
B	I	O	A	E	E	T	B	S	T	U	X	V	E	R	O	A	R	T	L
W	H	E	N	A	W	S	S	E	T	H	I	N	J	D	M	R	O	S	E
G	E	Y	U	N	B	H	D	E	P	D	R	E	M	E	S	G	A	B	R
D	R	J	A	T	I	R	E	A	D	O	R	L	X	P	I	C	C	E	N
C	L	N	O	I	R	A	M	S	E	L	A	N	E	X	H	M	M	I	O
E	R	G	S	H	I	I	X	E	W	C	I	C	H	R	O	M	E	L	H
C	H	E	M	E	L	W	F	A	O	E	T	W	L	I	U	I	N	H	A
Q	U	D	S	R	A	E	L	T	F	W	V	N	Y	S	A	T	E	T	P
I	N	K	L	O	E	R	D	F	W	Y	B	A	L	L	T	S	F	W	H
I	O	X	S	W	R	E	S	D	O	O	W	E	H	T	F	O	T	U	O
S	F	G	N	Z	E	A	E	S	H	H	U	W	B	S	J	L	I	S	A
E	D	D	A	N	E	D	R	V	N	R	R	O	S	S	I	A	D	B	N
A	G	R	U	D	D	Y	P	I	C	T	U	R	E	T	O	B	U	R	N
E	J	O	N	D	R	F	I	R	C	H	A	Y	E	B	E	Y	S	X	N
L	Y	E	T	J	X	O	R	H	I	F	K	D	R	C	E	N	A	E	F
I	L	N	W	F	A	R	P	F	E	A	H	C	N	U	R	T	O	P	S
E	L	A	T	Y	R	I	A	F	A	S	A	W	Y	A	D	O	T	A	T
C	H	U	E	D	G	T	N	X	K	E	R	C	H	R	D	O	D	Y	K

chapter 7

MASTERMIND

Taylor won a VMA for the video for the ten-minute version of "All Too Well," which appeared on *Red (Taylor's Version)*.

Forget girlboss; Taylor Swift is just a boss, period. She's one of the most successful recording artists of all time. Her last eleven albums have debuted at No. 1, most of them eclipsing a million copies sold in their first week. *The Tortured Poets Department* sold a tidy 1.5 million units in its debut week in 2024, the biggest album release since Adele's *25* in 2015, according to *Billboard*.

Six years earlier, in 2018, Swift ditched her former label, Big Machine, after a protracted fight to buy rights to the masters of her recordings ended with the label selling them out from under her. The saga of Big Machine, Scooter Braun, and Taylor's battle to get the rights to her music could fill the pages of this book and then some, but the short version bears repeating here because it is one of the most audacious and brilliant business moves that Taylor has made in her unparalleled career.

"For years, I asked, pleaded for a chance to own my work," Taylor wrote on social media. "Instead I was given an opportunity to sign back up to Big Machine Records and 'earn' one album back at a time, one for every new one I turned in. I walked away because I knew once I signed that contract, Scott Borchetta would sell the label, thereby selling me and my future. I had to make the excruciating choice to leave behind my past."

Borchetta indeed sold the label, and Taylor's catalog of work along with it, to a private equity firm for $300 million in 2019. Taylor signed a new deal with Universal/Republic Records, in which she retained the ownership of her masters, beginning with *Lover*. With her past work suddenly in the hands of a private investor, notorious uber-agent (and onetime Kanye West manager) Braun, Taylor was distraught.

"Let me just say that the definition of toxic male privilege in our industry is people saying, 'But he's always been nice to me' when I'm raising valid concerns about artists and their rights to own their music. And of course he's nice to you; if you're in this room, you have something he needs," she said

> **"This process has been more fulfilling and emotional than I could've imagined."**
>
> —Taylor on rerecording her previous work

at Billboard's Women in Music event in 2019. "The fact is that private equity is what enabled this man to think, according to his own social media posts, that he could 'buy me.' But I'm obviously not going willingly."

She didn't just get mad; she got even. Braun might have owned the original recordings, but he didn't own Taylor's words. Because Taylor has songwriting credits for every single song in her long career, she decided to rerecord them, album for album. "I just figured I was the one who made this music first; I can just make it again," she told *Late Night with Seth Meyers*. (The idea was reportedly first suggested to her by fellow artist Kelly Clarkson.)

What started as a stand on principle soon took on a life of its own. Swifties flocked to buy the rerecorded versions of their favorite albums as they trickled in one after the next. *Fearless (Taylor's Version)* and *Red (Taylor's Version)* were released in 2021. *Speak Now (Taylor's Version)* and *1989 (Taylor's Version)* were both released in 2023. All four of them debuted at No. 1 on the Billboard album charts.

Taylor's Versions provide more than just remixes. Each record is chock-full of bonus content, including tracks "From the Vault" that didn't make the initial cut

Taylor announces the release date of *198* *(Taylor's Version)* onstage at SoFi Stadium, Inglewood, California, in August 2023.

for their respective albums, and behind-the-scenes stories and other surprises.

It was a gutsy move by the artist that paid huge dividends. "You could imagine that this yearslong project might have culminated in a largely abstract victory over Braun that mostly just made a mess of Swift's catalog while also stalling her production of new songs," wrote The Ringer. But she has "managed to market her versions in a way that makes these old albums feel like new releases. Swift's obviously been a superstar for several years now, but she's only recently become something even grander—a multigenerational phenomenon on track to becoming the most popular artist in the history of streaming music."

The fact that the enthusiasm for *Taylor's Versions* has remained so high is extremely validating for the artist. And the cherry on top of this sundae, of course, is that she was able to leverage her influence in the industry to convince radio stations, including the giant conglomerate iHeartRadio, to go forward playing only *Taylor's Versions*, thereby devaluing the commodity that was purchased purely as a moneymaker. Now *that's* a master move!

If Taylor has been successful beyond her wildest dreams, it certainly isn't by luck. "No one is this good and works harder," said Jack Antonoff, her longtime collaborator and friend. Indeed, Taylor's work ethic is legendary.

Billion Dollar Baby

In December 2023, *Forbes* magazine published its annual list of wealthiest celebrities. Everyone expected Taylor to be on it (she was No. 25 on the list in 2022, with an estimated net worth of $570 million). A year later, she joined the Forbes Billionaires List with an estimated $1.1 billion net worth. That's a massive jump in just a year's time, but then consider everything she packed in: multiple hit albums (including two *Taylor's Versions*), a smash movie, and the most lucrative tour of all time. What's unique about Taylor is that as a performer she's amassed her wealth through music revenue, not the typical side hustles that so often goose a celebrity's fortune—fashion lines, cosmetics, and other business partnerships. In fact, *Forbes* reports that she's the first musician ever to become a billionaire solely from music.

Taylor is unique in that she's made most of her wealth on album sales and ticket revenue.

The Eras Tour is Taylor's love letter to fans around the world.

"Swift isn't just a great songwriter: She's an unparalleled marketing genius."

An unabashed feminist, Taylor believes that women have to work many times harder than their male counterparts. "The female artists that I know of have reinvented themselves twenty times more than the male artists. They have to, or else you're out of a job," she said in *Miss Americana*. "Constantly having to reinvent, constantly finding new facets of yourself that people find to be shiny" is a double standard in an industry that is already notorious for being predatory, according to Taylor.

Considering all this, it's little wonder that her post–Big Machine records address the dust-up with her formal label head-on. Taylor pointedly writes about it in songs such as *Folklore*'s "My Tears Ricochet" ("And when you can't sleep at night / You hear my stolen lullabies") and *Midnights*' "Vigilante Shit," as well as *Lover*'s "The Man," in which Taylor muses about how people would react to her career had she been a male rather than a female artist.

But as time marches on, it's clear that she's no longer a female artist in a man's world. As fellow trailblazer Barbara Walters put it, "Taylor Swift *is* the music industry." ★

Musical Questions (*Taylor's Version*)

With *Taylor's Versions*, Swifties have been treated to so many extra goodies, including bonus tracks. Can *you* score a perfect ten identifying these songs from the vault? Name the song from which the following lyrics have been taken.

1. *I lived, and I learned / Had you, got burned / Held out, and held on / God knows, too long.*

2. *You, who charmed my dad with self-effacing jokes / Sipping coffee like you're on a late-night show*

3. *She's the kind of book that you can't put down / Like if Cleopatra grew up in a small town*

4. *Don't you smile at me and ask me how I've been / Don't you say you've missed me if you don't want me again.*

5. *Why'd you whisper in the dark / Just to leave me in the night?*

6. *You won't believe half the things I see inside my head / Wait 'til you see half the things that haven't happened yet.*

7. *Let's fast forward to three hundred takeout coffees later / I see your profile and your smile on unsuspecting waiters.*

8. *How is it in London? / Where are you while I'm wonderin' / If I'll ever see you again?*

9. *On the counter was a cardboard box / And the sign said, "Photos: twenty-five cents each."*

10. *Oh, I hate those voices / Tellin' me I'm not in love anymore / But they don't give me choices / And that's what these tears are for.*

chapter 10

END GAME

TAYLOR SWIFT

Taylor's impact on pop culture is unprecedented. Some of the US's major news networks, including Gannett and *USA Today*, have hired dedicated Swiftie reporters. Major universities including Stanford, Rice, and Harvard offer courses on Taylor and her songwriting. And the Taylor Swift Effect has rippled across the film industry, the NFL, and even national economies (just to name a few), all of which have seen measurable boosts from the artist.

After such a monster year in 2023—crisscrossing the globe on her world tour, releasing multiple albums, breaking records across multiple industries—and with media saturation at full tilt, Taylor surely deserves a break.

But she shows absolutely no sign of stopping anytime soon.

The music keeps on coming. As of April 2024, she's entered the *Tortured Poets Department* era. Swifties have four of the six *Taylor's Version* albums—*Fearless*, *Red*, *Speak Now*, and *1989*—leaving only her debut record and *Reputation* left to rerelease.

The Eras Tour rolls on, with concert dates in Europe and North America continuing through December 2024, to the delight of Swifties on both sides of the globe.

Knowing Taylor, she's got a few extra tricks up her bejeweled sleeve too. And wherever she goes, Swifties are sure to follow. ★

Coming in Hot!

In 2022, Taylor achieved something no other artist in the history of the Billboard charts, which date back to 1940, had done. She broke the record for most consecutive songs at the top of the chart, holding the top ten spots with songs from *Midnights*. Not content to rest on her laurels, she broke her own record just two years later. In the first week of *The Tortured Poets Department*'s release, Taylor occupied the top fourteen spots on the charts. Overall, Taylor boasted nearly one out of every three songs on the Billboard Hot 100, with thirty-two separate tracks on the chart.

Lots going on at the moment, indeed.

Answers

Golden Girl (page 76)

1. C.
2. She won six awards in 2019, the *Lover* era.
3. She was nominated for Music Video of the Year for "I Bet You Think About Me."
4. None...yet.
5. She's been nominated for Best Original Song four times: for "Safe and Sound" from *The Hunger Games* (2013), "Sweeter Than Fiction" from *One Chance* (2014), "Beautiful Ghosts" from *Cats* (2020), and "Carolina" from *Where the Crawdads Sing*.
6. MTV Video Music Award for Best Video by a Female Artist. Bonus points if you knew it was for "You Belong with Me."
7. She won the Grammy in 2023 for the short film of the ten-minute version of "All Too Well."
8. C; she was not nominated for a Kids' Choice Award until 2010, with *Fearless*.
9. GLAAD.
10. D.

Star Search (page 109)

The hidden songs in the word search are "Anti-Hero," "Betty," "Cardigan," "Cruel Summer," "Enchanted," "Out of the Woods," "Picture to Burn," "...Ready for It," "Shake It Off," "Tim McGraw," "Today Was a Fairytale," "Wildest Dreams," and "You Need to Calm Down."

Musical Questions (*Taylor's Version*) (page 120)

1. "You All Over Me" (*Fearless*)
2. "All Too Well (10 Minute Version)" (*Red*)
3. "When Emma Falls in Love" (*Speak Now*)
4. "Don't You" (*Fearless*)
5. "Say Don't Go" (*1989*)
6. "I Can See You" (*Speak Now*)
7. "Is It Over Now?" (*1989*)
8. "Message in a Bottle" (*Red*)
9. "Timeless" (*Speak Now*)
10. "We Were Happy" (*Fearless*)

Taylor performs in her *Reputation* era.

"All I want to do is keep being able to do this. I love it so much. It makes me so happy. [And] it makes me unbelievably blown away that it makes some people happy [too]."